Wl

Gloria Steinem?

Who Is
Gloria Steinem?

By Sarah Fabiny

Illustrated by Max Hergenrother

Grosset & Dunlap
An Imprint of Penguin Group (USA) LLC

To all my Smith sisters—past, present, and future—SF

For Dr. Diane Hergenrother. You have shown by example
during your life and career that gender does not need to
determine the outcome of our goals. You are a great role
model, Mom—MH

GROSSET & DUNLAP
Published by the Penguin Group
Penguin Group (USA) LLC, 375 Hudson Street, New York, New York 10014, USA

USA | Canada | UK | Ireland | Australia | New Zealand | India | South Africa | China

penguin.com
A Penguin Random House Company

Text copyright © 2014 by Sarah Fabiny. Illustrations copyright © 2014 by Max Hergenrother. Cover illustration copyright © 2014 by Nancy Harrison. All rights reserved. Published by Grosset & Dunlap, a division of Penguin Young Readers Group, 345 Hudson Street, New York, New York 10014. GROSSET & DUNLAP is a trademark of Penguin Group (USA) LLC. Printed in the USA.

Library of Congress Cataloging-in-Publication Data is available.

ISBN 978-0-448-48238-5   10 9 8 7 6 5 4 3 2 1

Contents

Who Is
Gloria Steinem?

On June 4, 1982, over one thousand people attended a birthday party at the Park Avenue Armory in New York City.

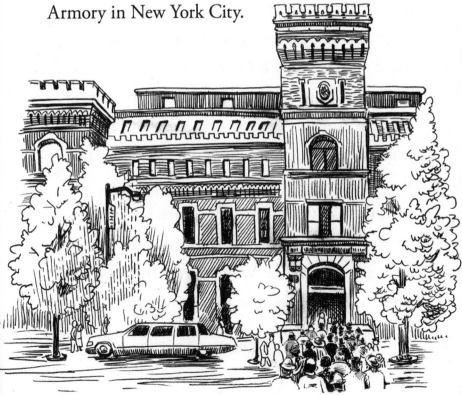

The birthday party wasn't for a person; it was for *Ms.* magazine. The magazine was celebrating its tenth birthday. But the partygoers weren't just there to celebrate *Ms.* They were there to honor the women who had started it—especially one woman in particular: Gloria Steinem. Gloria was the force behind the magazine. She had become the face of women's rights in the United States. When the magazine started, Gloria claimed she would only be there for two years. She wasn't sure she wanted to be involved longer than that. And she wasn't sure the magazine would last much longer than that, either. But after ten years, both Gloria and *Ms.* were going as strong as ever.

At the party, Gloria made a speech reminding the partygoers how far women had come since the magazine started. Women were no longer just housewives and mothers; they were astronauts, doctors, police officers, and even US Supreme Court justices.

The anniversary of *Ms.* was a proud moment for Gloria Steinem. She'd had a difficult childhood, yet Gloria was determined to improve her life— and she did. And she used that same  determination to help improve the lives of millions of women around the world.

Chapter 1
A Wandering Family

Gloria Marie Steinem was born in Toledo, Ohio, on March 25, 1934. Her parents, Leo Steinem and Ruth Nuneviller, had met at the University of Toledo in 1917. They both worked on the college newspaper. After college they married. Ruth taught college math for a year. It wasn't the career she really wanted. But she had promised her mother that she'd try teaching.

After a year, Ruth quit and got a job doing what *she* wanted to do. She became a reporter for the *Toledo Blade*.

At that time, people didn't think a woman could be as good of a reporter as a man. So Ruth used a man's name, Duncan Mackenzie, for her work at the newspaper. Ruth loved being a journalist, but she took a year off when their daughter Susanne was born in 1925.

Leo worked odd jobs after college. The year that Susanne was born he bought some land in Clarklake, Michigan. Clarklake was in a rural area about fifty miles northwest of Toledo. Leo built a resort in 1928. It was called Ocean Beach Pier. Leo hoped big-name bands would come and play for all the guests. But Leo's timing was bad.

The Great Depression hit in 1929, and many people lost their jobs. They weren't able to spend money on things like weekends dancing at a lake resort. In 1930, to help save money, the Steinems sold their house in Toledo and moved to Clarklake.

Ruth liked city life, and it was hard to give up her job at the newspaper. But she agreed to make a home at Ocean Beach Pier.

Soon after the move, Ruth gave birth to a baby boy who did not live long. That same year Ruth's father died, too. Lonely and isolated in the town of Clarklake, Ruth had a nervous breakdown. The medication she was prescribed helped, but she slept for hours when she took it. Ruth was no longer able to work or look after her children the way she once did.

THE GREAT DEPRESSION

THE GREAT DEPRESSION BEGAN ON OCTOBER 29, 1929, WHEN THE STOCK MARKET CRASHED, CAUSING MANY BANKS AND BUSINESSES TO SHUT DOWN. IT WAS THE WORST ECONOMIC CRISIS OF MODERN TIMES. UNEMPLOYMENT PEAKED IN 1933, WHEN ONE-QUARTER OF ALL AMERICANS WERE OUT OF WORK. MILLIONS OF AMERICANS LOST THEIR SAVINGS. LIFE WAS VERY DIFFICULT, AND MANY PEOPLE CAME TO DEPEND ON THE GOVERNMENT TO PROVIDE THEM WITH FOOD AND HOUSING. THE GREAT DEPRESSION LASTED NEARLY TEN YEARS. IT AFFECTED NOT ONLY THE UNITED STATES, BUT COUNTRIES ALL AROUND THE WORLD.

For years, Susanne had been begging for a baby sister. When Gloria arrived on March 25, 1934, everyone in the family was excited. Leo thought that perhaps a new baby would help make Ruth happy again. Ruth loved her new daughter, but she found it difficult to look after Gloria.

Gloria spent a lot of her childhood "running wild" at her family's resort in Michigan. She was free to play on the beach and catch turtles and minnows. She sometimes searched for coins that people had dropped in the lake. Gloria would also spend time in the dance hall watching the dancers and musicians. Ruby Brown, a dancer at the resort, taught Gloria how to tap-dance.

Gloria was pretty good at it, and once she learned the basic steps, she couldn't stop dancing. Gloria even dreamed of becoming a dancer when she grew up, just like Ruby.

Summers in Michigan were fun. But by October or November it was too cold for the Steinems to stay at the resort. The buildings didn't have heat. In the winter months, Gloria and her sister were taken out of school. Leo Steinem would pack up his family and they would drive to warmer places—California or Florida—in a trailer.

On the way, Gloria's father would make money buying and selling antiques. Ruth homeschooled Gloria and Susanne while the family was on the road. But the sisters were out of school for long periods of time and weren't learning as much as other children their age.

Gloria missed out on having friends and being involved in school activities. But she loved following her father around as he made his antique deals. Leo Steinem was fun and full of stories.

Leo also encouraged his daughters to be independent. Later in life, Gloria would say that her father treated her like a friend. He asked her advice and enjoyed her company. She also knew that she was loved, and her father honored her as a person. Gloria saw that some people in the world—like her father—believed that men and women and boys and girls weren't really so different. What mattered most was what a person could do.

Chapter 2
Her Mother's Keeper

Millions of troops are on the move...

Is YOUR trip necessary?

Even though the United States was recovering from the Great Depression in the early 1940s, there was still a shortage of gasoline due to World War II. This meant people weren't traveling as much. Ocean Beach Pier didn't have many visitors, so Gloria's father had to close it down. Leo and Ruth had to decide where to live, what to do for work, and how to raise their family. The stress of the situation was too much for Gloria's parents, and they divorced when she was ten years old.

Gloria and her mother moved from Clarklake to Amherst, Massachusetts, to be close to Susanne. She was attending Smith College, in nearby Northampton.

Leo moved to California, but he spent a lot of time on the road selling antiques. Gloria missed her father, who had been such an important person in her life. Although they wrote letters, they saw each other only once or twice a year.

Gloria was now in fifth grade, and she started to attend school regularly for the first time in her life. She was behind in math and science classes.

But she was bright, curious, and a good reader, so Gloria soon caught up with her classmates. Gloria also liked playing sports. She made friends easily and felt like she fit right in at school.

When Susanne began her last year of college, Gloria and her mother moved back to Toledo, Ohio, into the house where Ruth had grown up. The house had since been divided into apartments. Gloria and her mother moved into the apartment on the top floor of the house and rented out the rest.

The space Gloria shared with her mother was small and cramped. They shared bunk beds. The furnace was dangerous, and rats ran in and out of the cupboards.

Ruth's depression worsened. Gloria had to look after her mother. It was as if Ruth had become the child and Gloria had become the parent.

While she took care of her mother, Gloria attended Monroe Elementary School. Gloria loved reading, and her books became some of her best friends. They helped her escape the hardship of having to be her mother's caretaker. Gloria read books like *Gone with the Wind*, *A Tale of Two Cities*, and the Nancy Drew mysteries.

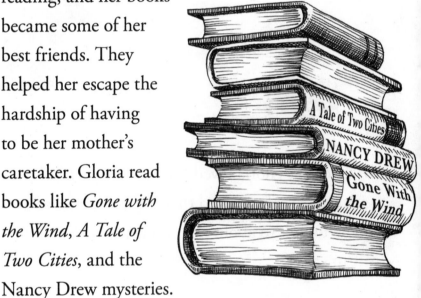

But her favorite book was *Little Women* by Louisa May Alcott. Gloria felt that she was like the character Jo, who had a great spirit of adventure and longed for independence.

Most of all, Gloria loved the "sisterly chats" the girls shared. She wished that she had someone at home to talk to about her problems, hopes, and dreams.

LITTLE WOMEN

LITTLE WOMEN, BY LOUISA MAY ALCOTT, WAS PUBLISHED IN 1868. IT TELLS THE STORY OF THE FOUR MARCH SISTERS— MEG, JO, BETH, AND AMY—AND THEIR LIVES IN NEW ENGLAND WHILE THEIR FATHER IS AWAY FIGHTING IN THE CIVIL WAR. ALTHOUGH THE FAMILY IS POOR, THEY ARE VERY

LOUISA MAY ALCOTT

LOVING. THE BOOK IS DIFFERENT THAN MOST BOOKS WRITTEN AT THE TIME IN THAT IT FOCUSES ON THE LIVES OF GIRLS, NOT BOYS. IT DESCRIBES HOW THE SISTERS GROW FROM CHILDHOOD TO WOMANHOOD. *LITTLE WOMEN* IS A STORY OF HOPE, HAPPINESS, AND THE NEED FOR FAMILY AND FRIENDS.

Chapter 3
Breaking Free

Despite having to constantly care for her mother, Gloria went on to Raymer Junior High and Waite High School. And when she was old enough, she found jobs to earn extra money. She worked as a salesgirl in a local store and as a magician's assistant. She read scripts and played records at a local radio station. Gloria also used her tap-dancing skills to perform at a local Eagles Club, where she earned ten dollars per show. Dancing gave Gloria confidence in front of audiences, something that would help her later in life.

Between school and work, Gloria found time to take ballet lessons and danced in concerts with the Toledo Orchestra. The area she lived in was a working-class neighborhood. But at school and at her different jobs, Gloria met people who were wealthier and lived in nicer parts of town.

Gloria began to realize that most of the girls and women in her own neighborhood didn't have many opportunities. Their choices in life were limited.

With just one year left of high school, Gloria's sister invited her to come and live with her in Washington, DC. She wanted Gloria to attend a much better high school there.

Gloria didn't want to leave her mother, but she did want a chance at a better life. Gloria and Susanne asked Leo if he would be willing to look after Ruth for a year. With a bit of coaxing, Leo agreed. He loved Gloria and knew that she deserved the opportunity to leave her dreary life behind.

So Gloria moved to Washington, DC, where she attended Western High School. It seemed like a different planet, a million miles away from Toledo, Ohio! Gloria's new high school focused on preparing students for college.

WESTERN
HIGH SCHOOL

Gloria went to parties and made new friends. She had fun, something that had been missing from her life back in Ohio.

Gloria was happy to finally have the life of a normal teenager. Having to work hard at such a young age made Gloria a mature, confident person. She was popular with her classmates. Gloria was elected vice president of the student council and the senior class. She also joined the archery club and French club, and she worked on the yearbook.

Although Gloria enjoyed school, she worried about getting into a top college. She had good grades in English, but her grades in math, French, and social studies were much lower. But Smith College, where Susanne had gone, accepted her! Gloria was looking forward to a brighter future.

SMITH COLLEGE

SMITH COLLEGE, IN NORTHAMPTON, MASSACHUSETTS, WAS FOUNDED IN 1871 BY SOPHIA SMITH. SHE HAD INHERITED A LARGE SUM OF MONEY, WHICH SHE USED TO FOUND A COLLEGE JUST FOR WOMEN. SOPHIA SMITH WANTED WOMEN TO HAVE THE SAME OPPORTUNITIES AS MEN. SHE FELT THAT WOMEN COULD GAIN POWER THROUGH EDUCATION. THE COLLEGE WOULD BE A PLACE WHERE THEY COULD LEARN VALUABLE SKILLS. WHEN SMITH COLLEGE OPENED ITS DOORS IN 1875, THERE WERE FOURTEEN STUDENTS AND SIX PROFESSORS. TODAY, THERE ARE MORE THAN 2,500 STUDENTS AND OVER 280 FACULTY MEMBERS.

Chapter 4
Finding Her Place in the World

Many of the young women at Smith had
grown up in families that had plenty of money.
They hadn't experienced any of the hardships that
Gloria had. But Gloria headed to Smith with an
open mind.

She had learned how to tell funny stories from
her father. She found a way to make her family
life sound fun and a bit crazy. Soon Gloria's "tales
of Toledo" became a way for her to entertain her
classmates and make friends.

Gloria also dressed differently than her
classmates. Most of them wore the standard
fashions of the 1950s: Bermuda shorts, kneesocks,
blouses with cardigans, and pearl necklaces.
But Gloria wore heavy eye makeup and lots of

inexpensive jewelry. She also had long nails, which were always manicured. Her classmates were fascinated with Gloria and her style. They often asked if they could borrow her clothes.

Gloria loved college from the moment she arrived. She was able to focus on schoolwork for the first time in her life. She didn't have to look after her mother, worry about money, and work at part-time jobs. Her grades soon improved. By the end of her sophomore year, Gloria was on the dean's list.

Smith College offered students the opportunity to study abroad in Europe for their junior year. Gloria applied to the program in Geneva, Switzerland, and was accepted. In the fall of 1954, she first went to France, where she stayed with a family in Paris to brush up on her French. Then she traveled on to the University of Geneva.

While she was there, Gloria studied history, law, and literature. Her favorite class was international law.

When her courses in Geneva were over, Gloria earned a scholarship to study at Oxford University in England for the summer. She took even more literature classes and studied politics as well.

In the fall of 1955, Gloria returned to Smith College for her final year. At the beginning of her senior year she met Blair Chotzinoff. Gloria had gone out on dates with other young men while at Smith, but Blair was different. He was a pilot for the Air National Guard, and he was funny and adventurous. And Blair fell hard for Gloria. He took her for plane rides on their dates,

and one time he even wrote "Gloria" in the sky over the Smith campus. He thought she was not only beautiful, but bright and witty and independent.

Before long, Gloria and Blair were engaged to be married. Most women in Gloria's class expected to get married, settle down, and start a family. But soon after getting engaged, Gloria became uncomfortable with her decision. What would marriage mean for her? She had put her difficult childhood behind her and gone to an excellent college. Would she be losing all she had gained?

Although she loved Blair, she worried that marriage would stop her from having a career. Gloria had only just found her freedom, and she did not want to lose it.

Gloria graduated from Smith College on June 3, 1956. She had gone from struggling with her grades to becoming one of the top students in her class. Her father, mother, and sister were there to see Gloria accept her diploma.

After graduation, everyone expected Gloria to focus on her upcoming wedding. But Gloria felt more and more uneasy about getting married. She wasn't ready to settle down.

Gloria decided to call off the wedding. She loved Blair, and the decision was a difficult one to make. She decided to attend a one-year program to study in India. It would be a chance to get away and spend some time on her own.

On February 4, 1957, Gloria arrived in Bombay (now called Mumbai), India. From there she traveled to New Delhi, where she would study at the University of Delhi. Kayla Achter, a classmate from Smith, was also in the program.

The scholarship lasted for three months. Afterward, Gloria and Kayla decided to travel together and explore India. Gloria found India, its culture, and its people fascinating. She became very interested in the teachings of

Mohandas Gandhi, an Indian leader who had helped India win its independence from the British in 1947. Gloria studied Gandhi's teachings of how to overcome oppression with nonviolence.

MOHANDAS GANDHI (1869–1948)

MOHANDAS GANDHI IS CONSIDERED THE FATHER OF THE INDIAN INDEPENDENCE MOVEMENT. HE WAS CALLED *MAHATMA*, MEANING "GREAT SOUL," BY THE PEOPLE OF INDIA. HE LED THE INDIAN NATION TO FREEDOM THROUGH HIS WORDS AND ACTIONS, NOT VIOLENCE OR WEAPONS. SOME OF HIS MOST IMPORTANT TEACHINGS ABOUT LEADERSHIP ARE:

- IF YOU DO SOMETHING THE PEOPLE CARE ABOUT, THE PEOPLE WILL TAKE CARE OF YOU.

- IF YOU WANT PEOPLE TO LISTEN TO YOU, YOU HAVE TO LISTEN TO THEM.

- IF YOU HOPE PEOPLE WILL CHANGE HOW THEY LIVE, YOU HAVE TO KNOW HOW THEY LIVE.

- IF YOU WANT PEOPLE TO SEE YOU, YOU HAVE TO SIT DOWN WITH THEM EYE TO EYE.

Gloria spent a month in Calcutta and then headed to the Madras region of India. There, she joined a group of Gandhi's followers who organized a walk to protest the caste, or class, system in India. As she traveled around the country, Gloria gained a better understanding of Indian society, especially how badly women and members of the poorer, lower castes were treated. Gloria began to think about her own country in a new way. She started writing articles about what she saw and how it made her feel about the role of women in America, as well as in India. She wanted her writing to help people back in the United States see society in a new and different way.

Before leaving India, Gloria wrote a travel guide called *The Thousand Indias*. It was published by the Indian government and was meant to attract Americans to study and travel in India. The guidebook became popular, and Gloria got more writing assignments. Her writing and other part-time jobs allowed her to stay in India for another year.

Gloria's time in India was a major turning point in her life. "Most of us," she later wrote, "have a few events that divide our lives into 'before' and 'after.' This was one for me."

Chapter 5
Finding Work

Gloria was sad
to leave India in
the fall of 1958, but
she was inspired
by the things she
had seen and done
there. She hoped to
use her experiences
and begin a career
as a writer. When
she returned to
the United States,
Gloria went to
New York City to
look for work.

Gloria was determined to find a writing job that would allow her to help improve the lives of others. By becoming a journalist, Gloria would be following in her mother's footsteps.

Gloria spent months searching for a job that interested her. She couldn't afford her own apartment, so she stayed with friends. Gloria applied for many jobs, but no one offered her a position. She discovered that serious topics were covered by male journalists. Female writers were expected to write articles on fashion and beauty.

Frustrated by her job search in New York City, Gloria moved to Cambridge, Massachusetts. There, she accepted a job as the director of the Independent Research Service in 1959. The Independent Research Service was a foundation funded by the US government's Central Intelligence Agency (CIA). It sent American students to youth festivals around the world. Their goal was to promote the American ideal of democracy. The foundation hoped that the American students would show how good life was in the United States. The Soviet Union, a communist country, was a very powerful nation. The US government was worried about communism, which did not allow its citizens a voice in their government, spreading to other parts of the world.

COMMUNISM AND THE COLD WAR

IN 1945, AT THE END OF WORLD WAR II, AMERICA AND THE SOVIET UNION WERE THE STRONGEST COUNTRIES IN THE WORLD. THE SOVIET UNION WAS A COMMUNIST COUNTRY, WHERE THE GOVERNMENT CONTROLLED THE ENTIRE NATION. THE UNITED STATES WAS A DEMOCRACY WITH ELECTED LEADERS. THESE TWO COUNTRIES BECAME KNOWN AS *SUPERPOWERS*. THE SUPERPOWERS NEVER ACTUALLY DECLARED WAR ON EACH OTHER. BUT THEY WERE ENEMIES. THE "COLD WAR" WAS THE NAME GIVEN TO THIS LONG PERIOD OF TENSION.

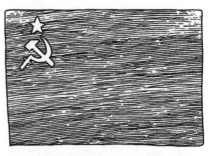

DURING THE COLD WAR, THE CENTRAL INTELLIGENCE AGENCY (CIA) COLLECTED INFORMATION THROUGH THE USE OF SPIES. THE SOVIET UNION ALSO USED SPIES TO COLLECT INFORMATION ABOUT THE UNITED STATES. THE COLD WAR LASTED FROM 1945 TO 1991, WHEN THE SOVIET UNION COLLAPSED.

Gloria did her job very well. She had a reputation as a smart, hard worker. But after the 1959 Youth Festival in Vienna, Austria, ended, so did Gloria's job. She moved back to New York City and was determined to make it as a writer.

Through friends, Gloria met Harvey Kurtzman, the founder of *Mad* magazine. Kurtzman was setting up a new magazine called *Help! For Tired Minds*. The magazine had funny articles and cartoons that poked fun at the US government and politicians. He hired Gloria to arrange interviews and photo shoots. It wasn't really a dream job, but it was a step in the right direction. Gloria's life was going well.

She was starting to find success as a writer. And she was finally able to move into an apartment of her own.

EZ-MOVING & STORAGE
DELUXE SERVICE FROM DOOR TO DOOR
SERVING THE PUBLIC SINCE 1924

On April 20, 1961, Gloria received the news that her father had been in a car accident in California. Sadly, he died before she was able to get there. Gloria had not been close to her father since her parents' divorce, but he had been an important person in her life.

Gloria continued to work in New York. She wrote articles for the *New York Times* and *Glamour* and *Harper's* magazines. *Ladies' Home Journal* published articles she had written about the actor Paul Newman and the singer Barbra Streisand.

In 1963, Gloria got her biggest writing assignment yet—which made her famous. *Show* magazine wanted to do an article on the opening of the Playboy Club in New York. It was the newest in a chain of nightclubs in the United States. Gloria never wanted her looks to be a factor in her writing career. But she knew that being young and pretty would help her with this

special—and secret—assignment. Gloria wanted
to expose how young women were working at jobs
no man would ever do. They were being treated
poorly as waitresses at the Playboy Clubs.

For a month, Gloria worked undercover at the
club in New York City. She wore the same uniform
as the other waitresses—thin, sheer stockings;
a tight, scratchy costume with a fluffy bunny tail;

high-heeled shoes; and
bunny ears. Gloria asked
the other waitresses as many
questions as she could.
She kept notes about how
uncomfortable the outfits
and shoes were, and how
poorly the waitresses
were paid. The
young women were
even told whom to
date! She knew that for
many pretty, uneducated
young women, this was
the best type of work they could find. Her
article appeared in *Show* magazine and brought
her instant fame. But it wasn't the kind of fame
Gloria wanted. People criticized her for the article.
They thought that a pretty woman working at
a Playboy Club wasn't really an important story.

Many people didn't understand why writing about Playboy Bunnies was even "news." After the Playboy article, many magazines wouldn't give Gloria work! They didn't think of her as a serious journalist.

But Gloria didn't let that stop her. She was determined to overcome this setback, just as she had overcome so many other things in her life.

Chapter 6
Finding Feminism

Up to this point, Gloria's journalism career had been a way to pay the bills. She still wasn't writing about issues that mattered to her. Issues like equality, injustice, the role of women, and racism. But even though she wasn't paid to report on these things, Gloria began working hard to make the world a better place.

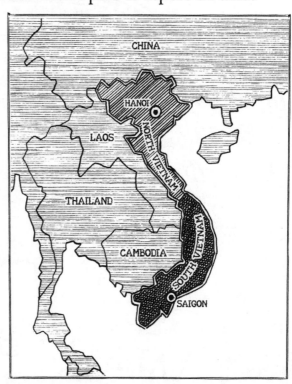

At the time, the United States was involved in the Vietnam War.

The US government had sent troops to help
South Vietnam stop North Vietnam from
combining the two parts into one communist

country. Many people did not want the United States to take part in the war. Gloria was one of them. In 1967, she marched in an antiwar rally in Washington, DC, called Women Strike for Peace.

Gloria also passionately supported the civil rights movement. When Martin Luther King Jr. was assassinated, Gloria went to Harlem. She visited this mostly African American neighborhood in New York City to learn how his death had affected the people there.

And Gloria's interest in women's rights was never stronger. Women's issues were becoming important topics in the 1960s. Betty Friedan, who had also gone to Smith College, had written a book called *The Feminine Mystique* in 1963. The book was getting a lot of attention.

In 1968, Clay Felker, a friend and colleague of Gloria's, left his job at *Esquire* magazine. He began developing a magazine called *New York* that focused on life in New York City. Clay hired a group of writers, including Gloria, to help him get the magazine started. He recognized Gloria's talent as a writer. He also knew that she understood politics. Gloria became *New York*'s political columnist.

THE FEMININE MYSTIQUE

BETTY FRIEDAN

IN 1957, BETTY FRIEDAN TOOK A SURVEY OF HER SMITH COLLEGE CLASSMATES FOR THEIR FIFTEENTH REUNION. THE RESULTS OF THE SURVEY REVEALED THAT MANY OF FRIEDAN'S CLASS-MATES WERE UNHAPPY WITH THEIR LIVES. THEY DID NOT ENJOY BEING HOUSEWIVES. THEY WANTED MORE OPPORTUNITIES AND FELT THEY COULD ACCOMPLISH MORE.

BETTY FRIEDAN DECIDED TO INTERVIEW OTHER SUBURBAN HOUSEWIVES. SHE ALSO STUDIED HOW WOMEN WERE PORTRAYED IN ADVERTISING AND MOVIES, AND ON TV.

HER BOOK, *THE FEMININE MYSTIQUE*, SHOWED THAT, WHILE THE MEDIA DEPICTED WOMEN BEING

HAPPY AS HOUSEWIVES, MANY WOMEN FELT TRAPPED IN THAT ROLE.

THE BOOK IS CONSIDERED ONE OF THE MOST IMPORTANT NONFICTION BOOKS OF THE TWENTIETH CENTURY. IT URGED WOMEN TO BECOME EDUCATED AND TO FIND WORK OUTSIDE THE HOME. BY DOING THIS, THEY WOULD GAIN A SENSE OF PURPOSE. THE BOOK HELPED SPARK THE BEGINNING OF THE SECOND WAVE OF FEMINISM IN THE UNITED STATES.

Finally, Gloria had the opportunity to cover subjects that she cared deeply about. She was determined to report on issues that affected women and other groups that weren't previously covered in important magazines.

Suddenly Gloria was covering big stories. She wrote about the presidential campaign, the Democratic National Convention, the struggles of the migrant workers' union, and the growing feminist movement.

Writing about important causes showed Gloria that women were far from being treated equal to men. And this frustrated her. The leader of the migrant workers' union, Cesar Chavez, thought women should remain wives and mothers. Women attending the Democratic National Convention were not even allowed to give speeches to delegates! And women working on the presidential campaign were still given the least important jobs.

In March 1969, *New York* magazine asked Gloria
to cover a rally. The rally was organized by an
outspoken feminist group called the Redstockings.

FEMINISM

FEMINISM IS THE BELIEF THAT WOMEN SHOULD HAVE THE SAME RIGHTS AS MEN. IT ALSO STATES THAT WOMEN SHOULD HAVE THE SAME ACCESS TO EDUCATION AND THE SAME WORK OPPORTUNITIES. THE "FIRST WAVE" OF FEMINISM IN THE UNITED STATES BEGAN IN 1848. THIS WAS THE YEAR ELIZABETH CADY STANTON AND LUCRETIA MOTT DRAFTED A DECLARATION OF SENTIMENTS BASED ON THE DECLARATION OF INDEPENDENCE. THE DECLARATION CALLED FOR WOMEN'S SUFFRAGE —THE RIGHT TO VOTE. IN 1869, STANTON AND SUSAN B. ANTHONY FOUNDED THE NATIONAL WOMAN SUFFRAGE ASSOCIATION TO SUPPORT THE CAUSE. IT TOOK MORE THAN *FIFTY YEARS* FOR THEIR WORK TO PAY OFF. IN 1920, THE NINETEENTH AMENDMENT TO THE US CONSTITUTION FINALLY GAVE WOMEN THE RIGHT TO VOTE. THE "SECOND WAVE" OF FEMINISM IS SAID TO HAVE

STARTED WHEN BETTY FRIEDAN PUBLISHED *THE FEMININE MYSTIQUE* AND COFOUNDED NOW (THE NATIONAL ORGANIZATION FOR WOMEN). WITH THIS NEW WAVE, FEMINISTS TURNED THEIR ATTENTION TO ISSUES SUCH AS EQUAL PAY FOR EQUAL WORK, AND MORE AND BETTER JOB OPPORTUNITIES.

ELIZABETH CADY STANTON
AND SUSAN B. ANTHONY

Gloria was just there to report on the meeting. But it turned out to be an eye-opening event for Gloria and a turning point in her life's work. Gloria listened to the Redstockings talk about their experiences as women. She realized *their* stories about having to overcome hardships and prejudice were also *her* story.

After the meeting, Gloria wrote her first feminist article for *New York*. It was called "After Black Power, Women's Liberation." She talked about how the civil rights movement and the women's rights movement should work together.

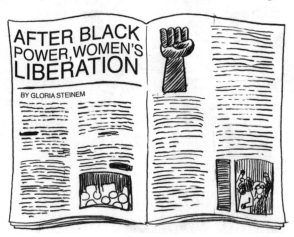

Gloria believed that if the two movements supported each other—black and white, men and women—they would both succeed. The article won the prestigious Penney-Missouri Journalism Award, as one of the first reports on the new wave of feminism in the United States.

But some of Gloria's male coworkers questioned her work. Why had she chosen to write about these "crazy women" instead of something serious and important? They asked her why she wanted to cover "women's stuff" when she had worked so hard to get "real assignments." For Gloria, women's rights *were* the most "real" assignment.

Those comments confirmed Gloria's dedication to the feminist movement.

From that point on, no one thought of Gloria Steinem without thinking of the word *feminist*. Gloria realized that she could also help spread the word about women's rights by speaking to people. It was a way to "get the word out" when many magazines and newspapers did not want to publish articles about feminism.

Gloria was sometimes nervous about speaking in public. But her desire to spread the word about feminism was stronger than her fear. In September 1969, Gloria spoke to the Women's National Democratic Club about her prizewinning article. She asked her friend Dorothy Pitman Hughes, an African American feminist, to speak with her. Hughes had opened a child-care center for working mothers—something that was rare in the 1960s. Gloria and Dorothy believed their partnership would show that the women's movement applied to all women, no matter their age or the color of their skin.

Chapter 7
A New Kind of Magazine

Gloria began receiving lots of invitations to speak to people. In May 1970, she spoke in front of the US Senate in support of the Equal Rights Amendment (ERA). She also spoke to the graduating class at Smith College in 1971, and at the *Harvard Law Review* banquet. People wanted to hear what Gloria thought and what she had to say. She was quickly becoming the spokesperson for the women's movement in the United States.

Part of the reason that Gloria stood out as a spokesperson was her look. Many people expected feminists to be plain and not very stylish. But Gloria Steinem was glamorous. Although she was a feminist, she didn't ignore her femininity.

She had highlights in her long hair, and wore
frosty pink lipstick and tinted aviator sunglasses.
She also wore flared jeans with wide belts and
turtlenecks. This look became Gloria's trademark,
and many women copied it.

ERA

THE EQUAL RIGHTS AMENDMENT WAS DRAFTED BY ALICE PAUL IN 1923. SHE WAS ONE OF THE FIRST LEADERS OF THE MOVEMENT FOR EQUAL RIGHTS FOR WOMEN IN THE UNITED STATES.

THE AMENDMENT STATES: "EQUALITY OF RIGHTS UNDER THE LAW SHALL NOT BE DENIED OR ABRIDGED BY THE UNITED STATES OR BY ANY STATE ON ACCOUNT OF SEX."

ALICE PAUL

THE AMENDMENT HAS BEEN BROUGHT BEFORE THE US CONGRESS EVERY YEAR SINCE IT WAS WRITTEN, BUT IT HAS NEVER PASSED. FEMINIST ORGANIZATIONS CONTINUE TO WORK FOR THE ADOPTION OF THE EQUAL RIGHTS AMENDMENT.

But not everyone was happy about all the attention that Gloria Steinem was getting—including Betty Friedan. Friedan had cofounded the National Organization for Women (NOW) in 1966. Its goal was to get women more involved in society and achieve equal rights with men. Most of NOW's members were white women who didn't have to struggle to earn a living. Gloria agreed with NOW's goals, but she thought the organization did not represent every feminist. Gloria felt that the women's movement should speak for women of every age, color, and class, whether rich or poor. After almost every talk she gave, Gloria would leave with pockets full of slips of paper. She had written the names and phone numbers of the women she had met on these slips. She wanted to speak to and help as many women as she possibly could. But with her

writing and her speaking, Gloria was very busy.
It was becoming impossible for her to do all the
things she wanted to.

Gloria wanted to reach out to as many
women as she could. She was eager to respond
to the antifeminism articles that were appearing
in magazines. So Gloria and some of her
colleagues decided to publish their own magazine.

The magazine would be special—it would be owned and run by women only. There hadn't been a magazine published just by women in the United States since 1868, when Susan B. Anthony and Elizabeth Cady Stanton published *The Revolution*.

As with so many other things in her life, Gloria did not let fear stop her. She believed in the idea of a women's magazine. And she and her friends were determined to make it happen.

Gloria asked her friend Clay Felker to help.

He offered to include a short sample of Gloria's magazine about women inside *New York*'s December 20, 1971 issue. The sample would be a test to see public reaction to the magazine. Gloria and her colleagues decided to call the magazine *Ms.* The term *Ms.* wasn't *Mrs.* or *Miss.* It didn't indicate whether or not a woman was married.

Ms. published its first full separate issue in January 1972. The magazine included articles about marriage and children, discrimination at work, and political issues such as the war in Vietnam. *Ms.* was an immediate hit. The 300,000 copies that were printed sold out in just  eight days. In just a few weeks, the magazine had 26,000 subscribers and had received more than 20,000 letters from readers!

With such a show of support, Gloria and her colleagues prepared to make *Ms.* a regular publication. Gloria's dream of creating a place where women could read about women's issues was taking shape. Women would have a chance to discover they were not alone in their concerns.

Chapter 8
Steps Forward and Back

Ms. magazine was a huge success with readers. Because of this success, Gloria and her colleagues wanted to help women's causes in other ways. In 1972, they created the Ms. Foundation for Women.

The foundation raised money for numerous women's causes, from helping abused women to supporting female politicians. At the time, there weren't many organizations that worked just to help women. Once again, Gloria was paving a new path for herself and all women.

Perhaps the most well-known project created by the Ms. Foundation is Take Our Daughters to Work Day. It was established to help girls experience firsthand all the work options open to them.

Gloria's schedule became even busier. She worked with the National Women's Political Caucus, which fought to help women get elected to political office. And she continued to fight for the passage of the Equal Rights Amendment. In 1972, *McCall's* magazine named her Woman of the Year.

TAKE OUR DAUGHTERS
TO WORK DAY

THE FIRST TAKE OUR DAUGHTERS TO WORK DAY WAS ON APRIL 22, 1993. IT WAS A SMALL EVENT THAT FIRST YEAR, BUT CURRENTLY MORE THAN 37 MILLION CHILDREN TAKE PART IN THE UNITED STATES ALONE. IT'S ALSO CELEBRATED IN COUNTRIES AROUND THE WORLD.

IN 2003, THE EVENT WAS EXPANDED TO INCLUDE SONS. THE EVENT IS NOW OFFICIALLY CALLED TAKE OUR DAUGHTERS AND SONS TO WORK DAY.

THE DAY IS CELEBRATED ON THE FOURTH THURSDAY OF APRIL EVERY YEAR.

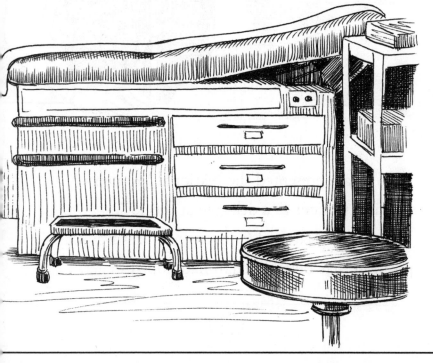

Gloria represented the National Women's
Political Caucus as a delegate at the 1972
Democratic National Convention. This was a
position that Betty Friedan had hoped to get.

The fact that Gloria was chosen fueled Friedan's
rivalry with Gloria. Friedan thought Gloria was
turning off women who enjoyed being married and
raising children. The Redstockings, the group that

helped raise Gloria's awareness of women's issues, also turned against her. They put out a press release that talked about the work Gloria had done for the Independent Research Service. The press release said that she had been associated with the CIA. The Redstockings claimed that Gloria had actually been "planted" by the CIA to gather information about feminists and the women's movement.

According to Betty Friedan and the women of NOW, Gloria was too extreme. To more radical women, like those in the Redstockings, Gloria was not extreme enough. These attacks hurt Gloria very much. She had dedicated much of her life to helping women and focusing attention on women's issues. And now she was being attacked because of it.

Another problem Gloria had to deal with was the advertising in *Ms.* Many advertisers did not want to place ads in a magazine that covered such controversial issues. So although *Ms.* magazine was popular with readers, they had to charge more for advertising than other magazines in the country. And because they had to charge more for advertising, they also had to charge more for the magazine. *Ms.* was more expensive than most magazines.

But Gloria had made a commitment to help women not only in the United States, but around the world, and she would not let them down.

In 1981, Gloria's mother, Ruth Steinem, died. Ruth's health had been declining, and she had been living in a nursing home. Although Gloria hadn't always had an easy life with her mother, she was very sad when she died. No one had been more proud of Gloria's achievements than her mother.

In 1982, *Ms.* magazine celebrated its tenth

anniversary. It was an incredible achievement. Gloria said, "It's a miracle that it managed to survive." The magazine had a party to celebrate, and the party was a big event. Bella Abzug, a former congresswoman from New York and a strong supporter of feminist causes, was at the party. She sang "Happy Birthday" for the partygoers.

Two years later, in 1984, Gloria celebrated her fiftieth birthday. Because she was so famous by then, over seven hundred guests attended her party! They included women who had influenced her, like civil rights pioneer Rosa Parks, and women who had benefited from her work, like astronaut Sally Ride.

The black-tie event was also a fund-raiser for the Ms. Foundation. It was a way for people to say "thank you" to Gloria. The party gave people the opportunity to show their appreciation for her tireless work.

Chapter 9
In It for Life

Gloria was already a successful journalist and speaker. But in the 1980s, her success as an author really took off. In 1983 she published *Outrageous Acts and Everyday Rebellions*. The book was a collection of some of her early writing about feminism. In 1986, she published *Marilyn: Norma Jeane*, a biography of Marilyn Monroe. It was the first biography of the movie star written by a woman.

In 1986, Gloria discovered that she had breast cancer. She later said that one of her first thoughts after her diagnosis was, "I've had a good life." But one thing was certain—Gloria's life was far from over. The same spirit she used to fight for women's issues she now used to get well.

Cancer did not slow Gloria down. She had surgery, underwent six weeks of radiation treatment, and then went on tour for her biography of Marilyn Monroe.

At first Gloria did not want anyone to know that she had breast cancer. She was treated under her grandmother's name, Marie Ochs. It wasn't until 1988 that she revealed she had cancer and spoke about her experience.

Revolution from Within: A Book of Self-Esteem was published in 1992. In it, Gloria wrote about her own life. The book showed people how they could use their past to help shape their future, just as Gloria had done. The response from women was incredible. Thank-you letters poured in and book signings drew huge crowds.

The book became a best seller. And in 1994, Gloria published *Moving Beyond Words*, a reflection on her own past and her thoughts on the future of feminism.

Over the years, the success of *Ms.* magazine helped other women's magazines to succeed. It also gave more mainstream magazines the confidence to publish feminist articles. But advertisers were still nervous about supporting feminist issues. They still wanted women's magazines to print traditional articles on fashion, beauty, and food. Because *Ms.* would not change the type of articles it published in order to get advertisers to pay for space in its pages, it stopped being profitable. The magazine was sold first in 1987, and then again in 1989. It was relaunched as an ad-free publication in 1990. This meant that the magazine was supported only by its readers. This allowed it to return to its feminist roots. By 1991, the magazine had once again become profitable.

Almost twenty years after founding *Ms.*, Gloria was able to devote less time and energy to the magazine. She was able to turn her attention to new things.

In 2000, at the age of sixty-six, Gloria got married. She surprised herself and many others with her choice. She said, "Though I've worked many years to make marriage more equal, I never expected to take advantage of it myself."

The man who became her husband was David Bale, a businessman and animal-rights activist. Instead of calling themselves husband and wife, they called each other "the friend I married." But sadly, after only three years of marriage, David Bale died of a brain lymphoma.

David's death was a horrible loss, but it didn't slow Gloria down. In fact, she dove into work. She continued to consult on *Ms.* and served on the board of trustees at Smith College.

And in 2005, she cofounded the Women's Media Center. The center promotes women's issues and stories about women in the media.

In her book *Outrageous Acts and Everyday Rebellions*, Gloria wrote an essay explaining how she came to devote her life to women's rights. She said, "In my first days of feminism, I thought I would do this ('this' being feminism) for a few years and then return to my real life (what my 'real life' might be, I did not know) . . . But like so many others now and in movements past, I've learned that this is not something we care about for a year or two or three. We are in it for life—and for our lives."

Gloria Steinem has spent her life working to improve the lives of women and making sure they have every opportunity they are entitled to. For Gloria, there is always more work to be done in the fight for equality. In her words, "We haven't even begun to imagine what could be."

TIMELINE OF
GLORIA STEINEM'S LIFE

1934 ——Born March 25 in Toledo, Ohio

1944 ——Parents divorce

1951 ——Moves to Washington, DC, to live with her sister, Susanne

1956 ——Graduates with honors from Smith College

1957 ——Studies in India

1959 ——Attends International Youth Festival in Vienna, Austria, for the Independent Research Service

1960 ——Moves to New York City

1961 ——Father dies

1963 ——Goes undercover as a Playboy Bunny at the Playboy Club in New York City

1968 ——Hired by *New York* magazine as political columnist and features writer

1972 ——Helps found *Ms.* magazine and the Ms. Foundation

1981 ——Mother dies

1986 ——Diagnosed with cancer

1993 ——Inducted into the National Women's Hall of Fame

2000 ——Marries David Bale

2003 ——David Bale dies

2005 ——Cofounds Women's Media Center

TIMELINE OF THE WORLD

World War II begins	1939
Mount Rushmore declared finished	1941
Ballpoint pens go on sale	1944
World War II ends	1945
Polio vaccine created	1952
School segregation ruled illegal in the United States	1954
Valentina Tereshkova becomes the first woman in space The March on Washington for Jobs and Freedom takes place in Washington, DC President John F. Kennedy assassinated	1963
National Organization for Women (NOW) founded	1966
Margaret Thatcher becomes first woman prime minister of Great Britain	1979
Sandra Day O'Connor appointed first woman US Supreme Court Justice	1981
Sally Ride becomes the first American woman in space	1983
Nelson Mandela freed from South African prison after twenty-seven years	1990
Terrorist attacks on the World Trade Center in New York City and the Pentagon outside Washington, DC	2001
Barack Obama elected president of the United States	2008

BIBLIOGRAPHY

* Attebury, Nancy Garhan. **Gloria Steinem: Champion of Women's Rights**. Minneapolis, MN: Compass Point Books, 2006.

Heilbrun, Carolyn G. **The Education of a Woman: The Life of Gloria Steinem**. New York: Ballantine Books, 1995.

* Lazo, Caroline. **Gloria Steinem: Feminist Extraordinaire**. Minneapolis, MN: Lerner Publications Company, 1998.

* Wittekind, Erika. **Gloria Steinem: Women's Liberation Leader**. Edina, MN: ABDO Publishing Company, 2011.

* Books for young readers

WEBSITES

Biography.com:
www.biography.com/people/gloria-steinem-9493491

Jewish Women's Archive:
jwa.org/encyclopedia/article/steinem-gloria

Makers.com:
www.makers.com/gloria-steinem